IMAGES
of America

KANSAS CITY'S HISTORIC HYDE PARK

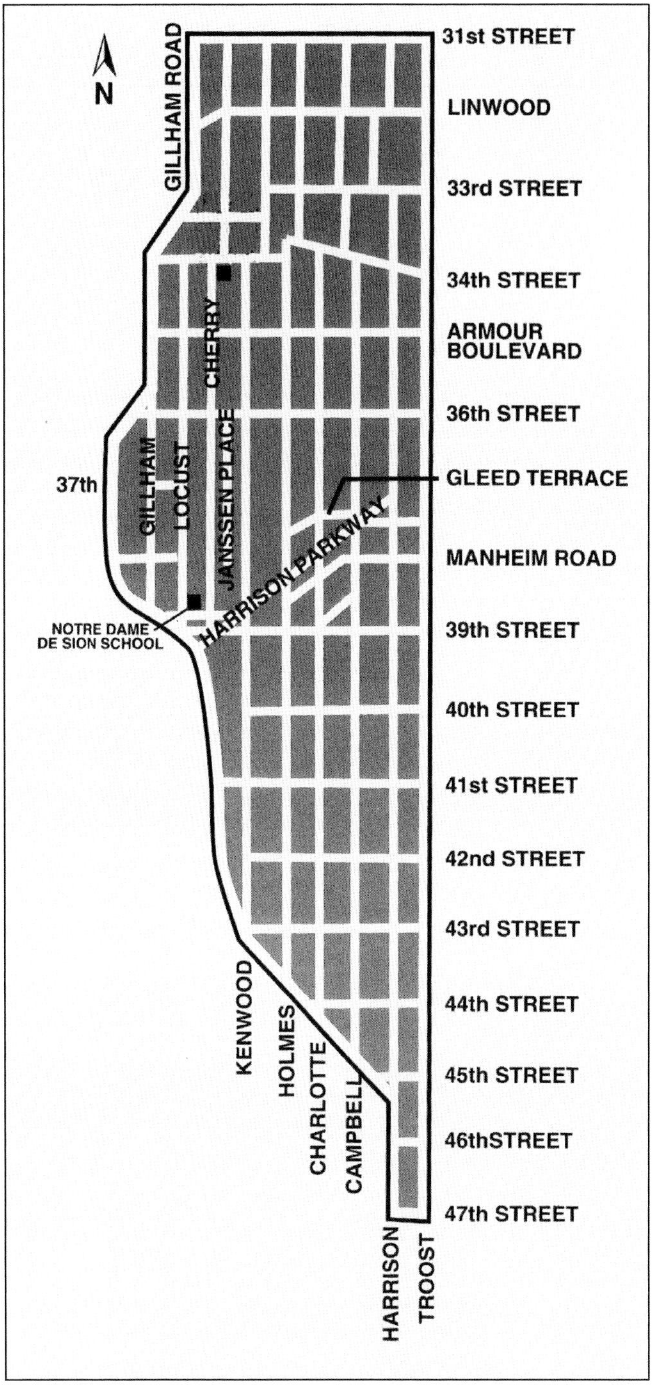

The Hyde Park neighborhood extends from Thirty-first Street on the north to Forty-seventh Street on the south and from Gillham Road on the west to Troost Avenue on the east. The numbered streets run east and west. The named streets run north and south, except Armour and Linwood Boulevards, Gleed Terrace, and Manheim Road. (Courtesy of Dona R. Boley.)

On the Cover: The popular fly-casting pool at Forty-first Street and Gillham Road, designed by George E. Kessler in 1913 and enlarged in 1940, gave locals a place to practice casting without having to leave town. On certain days, the facility was reserved for children as a wading pool. The casting pool was removed in 1976. (Courtesy of Missouri Valley Special Collections, Kansas City, Missouri Public Library.)

IMAGES
of America

Kansas City's Historic Hyde Park

Patrick Alley and Dona Boley for the
Hyde Park Neighborhood Association

ARCADIA
PUBLISHING

ISBN 978-0-7385-8850-6

Published by Arcadia Publishing
Charleston, South Carolina

Printed in the United States of America

Library of Congress Control Number: 2012930088

For all general information, please contact Arcadia Publishing:
Telephone 843-853-2070
Fax 843-853-0044
E-mail sales@arcadiapublishing.com
For customer service and orders:
Toll-Free 1-888-313-2665

Visit us on the Internet at www.arcadiapublishing.com

Contents

ACKNOWLEDGMENTS

In preparing this book, we have had extensive cooperation and help from many people and institutions. We want to thank everybody who gave us suggestions, brought us pictures, or shared stories or ideas.

First, we want to thank the archivists: Ann McFerrin of the Kansas City, Missouri, Parks and Recreation Department and David Jackson of the Jackson County Historical Society. The Kansas City Public Library and the Historic Kansas City Foundation gave us generous use of their resources. Many organizations loaned us photographs, including the Athenaeum Club of Kansas City, St. James Catholic Church, Central Presbyterian Church, Pilgrim Chapel, and Notre Dame de Sion School.

Many Hyde Park residents provided treasured photographs, including Steve and Barbara Mitchell, Doug and Susan Borge, Marsha Depping, Catherine Thompson, Paul Stevermer, Linda Becker, Kate McNeive, Cecelia Dillon, Roger Coleman, David Disney, and Pam Gard. Jane Foltz had a marvelous collection of family snapshots from the early 20th century, when her grandfather lived in Hyde Park.

Several people shared their ideas for content and helped with the editing, and our thanks go out to Steve Mitchell, Matt Levi, and Larry Hunter-Blank. Also, special thanks go out to Erica and Justin Grindley and Brad and Marilyn Rine, who all live far from Kansas City but were quick to share their collection. We would also like to thank Clif Hall of Photographic Creations. While living here, he served as the unofficial photographer of the Hyde Park Neighborhood Association. This book would not have been possible without his vast collection. Finally, we want to thank the Hyde Park Neighborhood Association board members for their support.

Photographic sources are abbreviated as follows:
ARL-JCHS: Archives and Research Library, Jackson County Historical Society
AWSE-HKCF: As We See 'Em, Historic Kansas City Foundation
BPRC: Board of Parks and Recreation Commissioners, Kansas City, MO
DRB: Dona R. Boley
HKCF-HUD: Historic Kansas City Foundation, under HUD funding
HPC-KCMO: Historic Preservation Commission, City of Kansas City, Missouri
HPNA: Hyde Park Neighborhood Association
Library of Congress: Library of Congress Prints and Photographs Division, Washington, DC
MVSC-KCPL: Missouri Valley Special Collections, Kansas City, Missouri Public Library
PA: Patrick Alley
PC: Photographic Creations
SBM: Stephen and Barbara Mitchell

INTRODUCTION

Kansas City was growing and growing fast. The population increased by over 35 percent in the last decade of the 19th century and then increased again 54 percent in the first decade of the 20th century. The trains moved people west, and the goods that they need followed close behind. The new settlers on the Great Plains shipped their cattle and grains to the eastern markets. Kansas City became a trading hub for most of the rich farmland and cattle ranches to the West. Banks multiplied, as the agriculture and building industries required expansion capital. The Ozark forests provided wood needed for building houses on the plains, and Kansas City was ready to deliver that lumber to its destinations. By 1900, Kansas City had become the largest city between St. Louis and San Francisco.

In the mid-1880s, real estate speculation in Kansas City reached frenzied proportions. Land south of Kansas City, extending to the town of Westport three miles distant, was sold and resold at fantastic profits. In 1887, real estate transactions in Kansas City were $88 million, and they would not reach that level again until 1946.

Platted in 1886, the Hyde Park subdivision was located between Kansas City and Westport, west of Gillham Road and outside the present-day boundaries of the Hyde Park neighborhood. On the east side of Gillham Road, Kenwood, Hampden Place, and several smaller subdivisions were already platted. Kansas City's first and only private street was laid out at this time when an upscale development called Janssen Place was platted. The Hyde Park area was the largest planned development of single-family homes in Kansas City until J.C. Nichols built his Country Club residential and shopping district in the 1920s

Hyde Park was greatly affected by the land boom of the 1880s. Seven additional subdivisions were platted in frantic succession from 1886 through 1888 with such sterling names as Nicolett Place, Edna Place, Hampden Place, and Regents Park. Fantastic speculation drove up land prices until the bottom dropped out after 1888 and development effectively halted for the next 10 years. Although the first houses were built in the late 1880s, less than 50 houses were constructed by 1900. However, by 1907, when the housing market had recovered, the number of homes increased more than five times. By the early 1920s, most of the houses in the area had been built.

Between the Hyde Park neighborhood and the eastern subdivisions lay a ravine and small creek. The old Independence-Westport wagon road used by Santa Fe and Oregon Trail travelers ran to the south. The nine-acre grassy gully between McGee and Oak Streets became the genesis of the park system surrounding the area. The land was first purchased for use as a private country club. The city eventually bought the property and added it to parkways created along Gillham Road and Harrison Parkway.

For many years, the entire residential area was generally referred to as Hyde Park without reference to any specific subdivisions. Today, the Hyde Park neighborhood only refers to the area east of the original Hyde Park subdivision. The Hyde Park neighborhood is now the area from

Thirty-first Street south to Forty-seventh Street between Gillham Road and Troost Avenue. There are approximately 2,000 homes in the area.

Three styles of architecture predominate: Colonial Revival style in brick, stone, and occasionally wood frame; Kansas City shirtwaist style, typified by a stone or brick lower story and a frame upper story, often with a bellcast gabled roof; and Bungalow style. Other styles represented are Victorian Romanesque, Queen Anne, shingle, American Foursquare and Prairie School. Many roofs are tile, and most garages or carriage houses are detached. Most of the houses have ornate hardwood interior trim, and many feature decorative plaster ceilings and leaded or stained glass.

In the late 1910s through 1920s, fashionable apartment hotels were built along Armour Boulevard in one of the highest concentrations outside of the downtown area. The Georgian Court, at Armour Boulevard and Gillham Road, contained only 24 units in its nine floors, and each seven- to nine-room suite rented for $375 per month in 1920.

By the end of World War II, a profound change had occurred in the area. Most original owners had passed away or moved south to the newer affluent communities. The large old homes were converted into apartments and sleeping rooms. The neighborhood began a slow decline that continued unchecked until the 1970s.

Since then, dramatic changes have taken place. An estimated one-third of the houses changed ownership between 1975 and 1977. Extensive public and private investments and attendant publicity revitalized the neighborhood. Most of the houses have been converted back to single-family homes, and once more the neighborhood has become an appealing place to live. Families walk the tree-lined streets with pets and relax on front porches. Today the brass fixtures shine, the leaded glass sparkles, and the woodwork glows.

One

The Early Years

In 1833, John Calvin McCoy built the first general store and trading post southwest of Independence, Missouri, and three miles south of the Missouri River, calling it "West Port." Positioned along the Santa Fe Trail on what is now the corner of Westport Road and Pennsylvania Street, it became a flourishing trading center among Indians, trappers, and the westbound adventurers. The new village was platted in 1834 around McCoy's store. To further enhance access, McCoy cleared a three-mile road from his small village to a rock outcropping on the south side of the Missouri River where it turns sharply to the north. The road effectively placed McCoy's new port on the farthest western point accessible to boats bringing goods up the Missouri from St. Louis. In 1834, the *John Hancock* was the first steamer to stop at McCoy's port, called Westport Landing.

With the discovery of gold in California in 1848, the trickle of hunters and trappers in the area became a torrent of fortune hunters eager to strike it rich. Over 100,000 people are estimated to have headed west by way of the Oregon Trail. Most of them stopped in Westport, the last stop to the western frontier. Westport incorporated in 1857. All three trails to the west could be accessed from the new town: the Oregon Trail, the California Trail, and the Santa Fe Trail. The small village soon became an ideal place for settlers to stop, refresh livestock, and buy last-minute necessities before continuing the long wagon journey west. Just east of the village was a natural spring and open grassland.

On July 3, 1869, the first railroad crossed the Missouri River on the Hannibal Bridge at downtown Kansas City. Soon after, growth in the town of Kansas City exploded. At the same time, Westport expanded east as far as Troost Avenue and north to present-day Thirty-first Street, but the growth of Kansas City soon reached Westport, and the two municipalities merged. While Westport eventually was incorporated by Kansas City, it retained its distinct, historical identity over the years. Kansas City became the hub of commerce for the Great Plains, first receiving cattle from the western ranchers and later grain from farmers. Soon, Kansas City provided timber, farm implements, and seed to the new settlers, who flooded into the plains as the railroads built westward. Kansas City's population increased from 2,500 in 1853 to 32,000 by 1870.

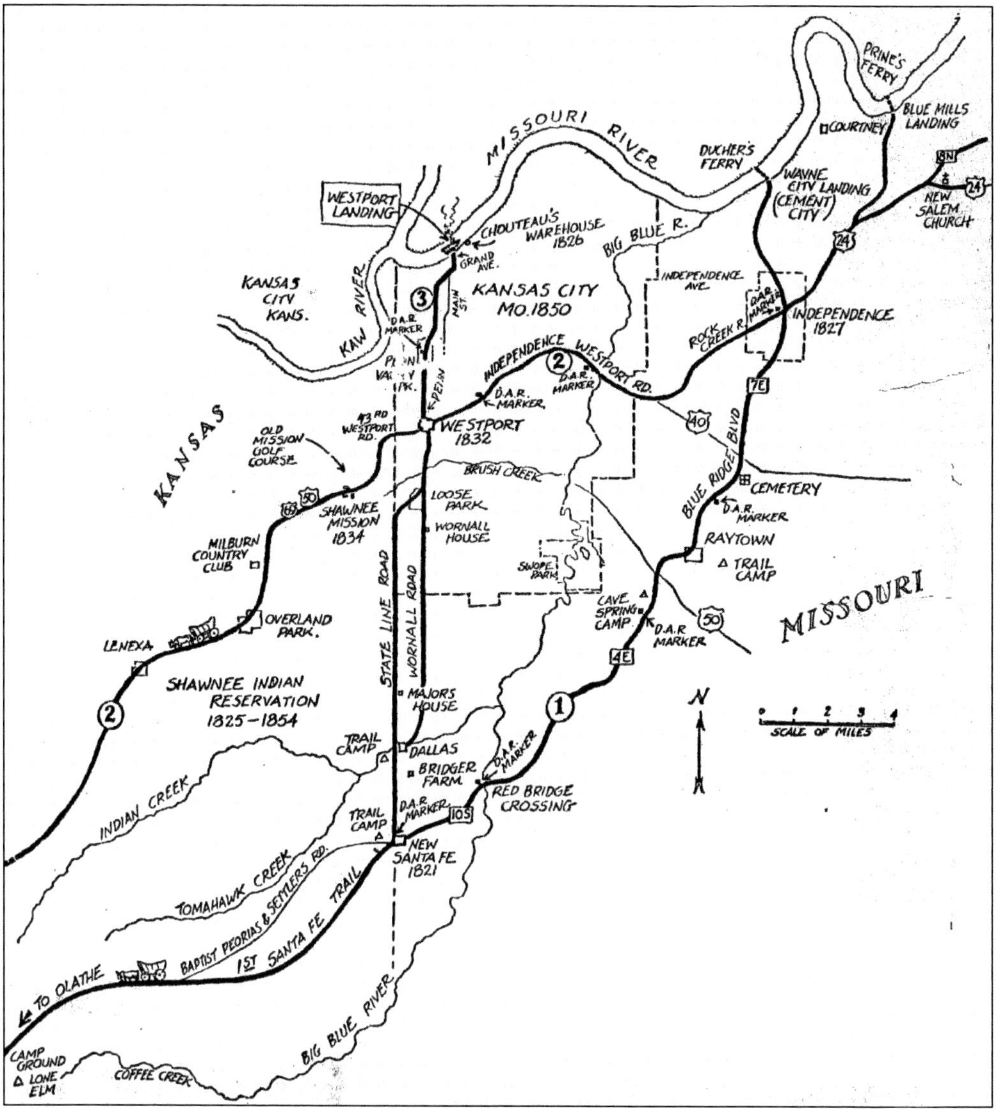

This map shows the 1832 route connecting Westport to Independence (2). Goods destined westward went by steamboat up the Missouri River to Blue Mills Landing or Wayne City Landing in Independence or, after 1835, to McCoy's Westport Landing (3). Once at Westport, travelers and trade goods could travel west or south to connect with the Santa Fe Trail. Blue Ridge Boulevard was another trail leading to the Santa Fe Trail (1). (Courtesy of ARL-JCHS.)

This photograph was taken in 1892 facing the northwest corner of Westport Road and Pennsylvania Street. This point was the epicenter of Westport during the 1850s. Westport Road runs west to the California and Santa Fe Trails. (Courtesy of MVSC-KCPL.)

The dirt road in the center of the photograph is a small remnant of the trail connecting Independence, Missouri, to Westport. Gillham Road is in the foreground near Thirty-ninth Street. Down the hill from the road, back toward the tree line, is one of the freshwater springs. (Courtesy of BPRC.)

This photograph, facing south from Thirty-ninth Street, was taken in August 1904, before the area developed. It depicts the open nature of the land that allowed the wagons to circle and form a holding pen for livestock. Streams and springs provided fresh water. (Courtesy of BPRC.)

The only remains of Cave Springs, as this area was known in 1850, are a small bog and the rim of the limestone outcropping. Local legend says Jesse James hid in the cave when he passed through the area. The city blocked the cave entrance as a safety measure. This photograph faces north to the intersection of Gleed Terrace and Charlotte Street. (Courtesy of PA.)

Two

Janssen Place

By the late 1880s, Kansas City was in the midst of a major real estate boom. The wealthy residents had moved south, away from the shantytowns along the river bottoms and the stench of the stockyards and meatpacking companies that had made them rich.

Arthur Stilwell, founder of Kansas City Southern Railroad, owned a house on East Thirty-sixth Street (formerly Humbolt Avenue). Looking south from his front porch into the brush and trees of the undeveloped land south of Westport, he envisioned a planned neighborhood restricted to the wealthiest Kansas City citizens wishing to flee city squalor. He organized the Janssen Place Land Company and on July 14, 1897, introduced the plat of Janssen Place. The subdivision's name honored August Janssen, a Dutch capitalist who had provided Stilwell significant financial backing for the railroad.

The land company purchased the Janssen Place site for $100,000. It comprised 32 lots, most 75 feet wide by 250 feet deep, but a few houses were constructed on more than one lot. A broad, private boulevard bisected the property north to south, lending a formal, symmetric aspect. Land-use covenants forbade the construction of fences between the properties, and each house was required to cost no less than $10,000.

The housing market was only just recovering from the financial panic of 1893, and buyers still considered Janssen Place too far away from the city. By 1906, only four Janssen Place lots had sold, and Stilwell dissolved the Janssen Place Land Company. W.P. Patton, a local investor, acquired the remaining lots and between 1907 and 1917, a total of 16 more lots sold.

Arthur Stilwell was born in Buffalo, New York, in 1859 and moved to Kansas City with his wife, Jennie Wood, in 1879. He worked in various professions, including insurance sales, before starting work in the rail industry. He founded the Kansas City Southern Railroad. He was the original developer of Janssen Place. He died in 1928. (Courtesy of MVSC-KCPL.)

Arthur Stilwell's house was directly across the road from Janssen Place. The design combined Victorian and shingle styles. The young lady standing in front of the house's entrance, on the east side of the facade, is unknown. Many Hyde Park families of this era kept livestock for meat, dairy, and egg products. (Courtesy of HKCF-HUD.)

Arthur Stilwell was a 19th-century entrepreneur. He developed more than 40 corporations, which established and controlled railroads, terminals, and other businesses along his railroad line. The city of Port Arthur, Texas, was named after Stilwell. (Courtesy of AWSE-HKCF.)

The White family, who lived across the street, is shown in this c. 1897 photograph of the Janssen Place entrance. Home construction had not yet begun. (Courtesy of HKCF-HUD.)

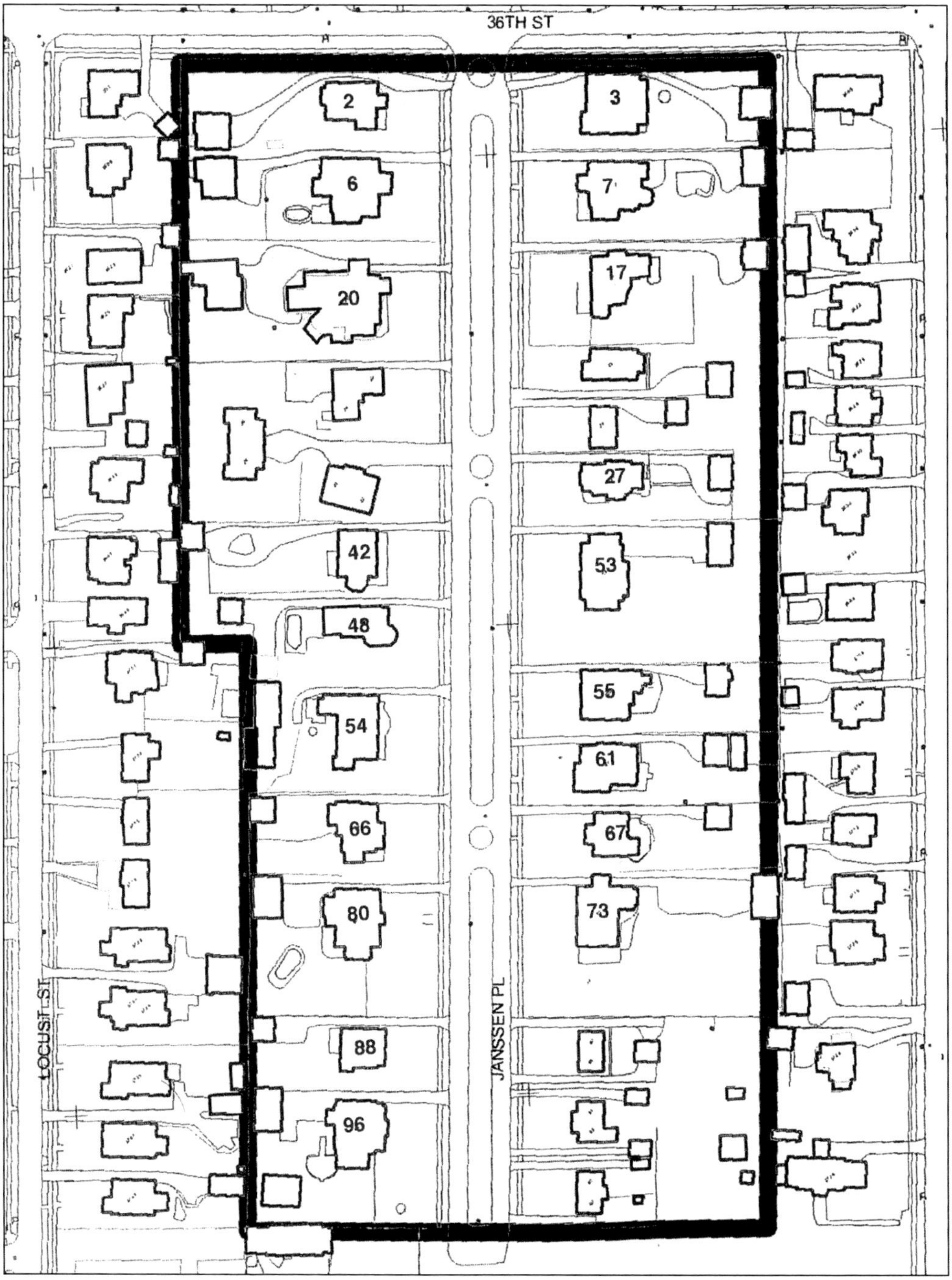

Of the 32 original lots from the 1897 plat, 20 sold by 1917. Because over half the mansions were built by businessmen owing their fortune to the lumber or construction industries, Janssen Place earned the nickname "Lumberman's Row." (Courtesy of DRB.)

The Neoclassical Revival–style entrance to Janssen Place is at the north end of the divided street. Erected in 1897, the portal was constructed of white Arkansas limestone. Large pillars frame an entablature supported by three Ionic columns containing the words "Janssen Place." (Courtesy of SBM.)

Life in Janssen Place was genteel. All the homeowners employed servants. Residents enjoyed the quiet open spaces, suitable for croquet, lawn tennis, and bridge club. Many households kept a cow for fresh milk and butter. This Hall Bros. postcard dates to around 1915. (Courtesy of SBM.)

Shown above is a detail of an entrance pillar. Arthur Stilwell hired local landscape architect George Mathews to design the Janssen Place grounds and entrance. Mathews also designed the Lyceum Building at 102–106 West Ninth Street, which was Stilwell's railroad office. Mathews died in 1903 at age 43 in a streetcar accident. (Courtesy of PA.)

The Queen Anne Victorian residence at 27 Janssen Place was the first house built in the subdivision in 1897. The three-story home was constructed with cut limestone on the first floor and cut slate shingles covering the second and third floors. The first owner was William A. Williams, a leader in the Kaw Valley Construction Company. (Courtesy of PA.)

Robert M. Rigby, a subsequent owner of 27 Janssen Place, was president of a local printing company. He came to Kansas City in 1879. At one time, his company employed 110 people and had an annual revenue of $200,000. Rigby had considerable income property and other interests, especially a love of fine horses. His horses included Sunny Slope, who had a trotting record of 2:10:25; trotting mare Jannetta C; and Howe Lambert, a fast road horse. (Courtesy of AWSE-HKCF.)

John Henry Tschudy built the home at 2 Janssen Place in 1905. The architectural firm of Howe, Holt, and Cutler designed the Italianate Revival home. The design of the home also has Arts and Crafts and Victorian influences. (Courtesy of PA.)

At right is a caricature of John Henry Tschudy taken from *As We See 'Em*, a volume of cartoons and caricatures of prominent Kansas City residents from about 1908. (Courtesy of AWSE-HKCF.)

John Henry Tschudy started the Tschudy Hardwood Lumber Company in 1887 and owned expansive hardwood forests in Arkansas. He died at age 79 on October 5, 1930, at his 2 Janssen Place home. (Courtesy of SBM.)

Anna Eggar married John Henry Tschudy in 1875. This picture dates to about 1880. When the Tschudy family moved into 2 Janssen Place, they had six children. Anna Tschudy died on December 16, 1940, at age 84 at home. (Courtesy of SBM.)

John Henry Tschudy's oldest daughter, Anne Tschudy, lived in the 2 Janssen Place house with two unmarried brothers until around 1947. In later years, Tschudy's daughter Mary Barbara reminisced that "Everyone knew his neighbors and entertaining was done in our homes. There was horseback riding on the country roads that then lay just south of us. It was an entirely different kind of living and would seem very slow to this generation." (Courtesy of SBM.)

The home at 3 Janssen Place is an Italianate Revival style, with typical pillar and brick decoration, third-floor balcony, and hooded molding over second-floor windows. George W. Ultch, owner of the Ultch Lumber Company, built the house in 1912. The architectural firm was Shepard, Farrar, and Wiser. (Courtesy of PA.)

Albert W. Peet built 6 Janssen Place in 1909. Peet's company, Peet Brothers Manufacturing, specialized in laundry, toilet soap, and glycerin. The company eventually became part of Colgate, Palmolive, Peet. This home is an excellent example of the Tudor-Jacobethan Revival style. The high-pitched gabled roof, elaborate chimneys, decorative half-timbering on the gables, and front-facing gables are evocative of the style. (Courtesy of SBM.)

This Italianate Revival home at 7 Janssen was built for Rodella G. Dwight in 1909 and completed in 1910. Kansas City architect John W. McKecknie designed the house. (Courtesy of PA.)

The home at 17 Janssen Place is of Tudor-Jacobethan Revival style and was designed by the local architectural firm of Shepard, Farrar, and Wiser. Abram Rosenberger, an associate of the H.M. Jones Distillery Company, built the house in 1912. (Courtesy of HPNA.)

William A. Pickering was the original owner of 20 Janssen Place. Pickering was vice president of Pickering Lumber Company, one of the largest lumber companies in the United States. The Italianate Revival style house had an Italian-style garden, complete with fountain, pool, and pergola. Behind the Italian garden was a rose garden with over 600 different varieties, most of them hybrid tea roses. (Courtesy of HPNA.)

Another lumberman, Joseph Mariotte Bernardin, built this Neogeorgian-style home in 1910 at 42 Janssen Place. The owner of the Bernardin Lumber Company, he was also a director at the Kansas City Federal Reserve Bank. The front porch and dormer windows are very typical of the Colonial style. (Courtesy of PA.)

The second house built in the subdivision was 48 Janssen Place. Burton D. Hurd, president of the Joseph O'Leary Machinery Company, purchased the house, constructed in Victorian and shingle styles, in 1900. The asymmetrical, circular side porch reflects a resort-town style that carries into the interior of the house. (Courtesy of PA.)

The architectural firm Keene and Simpson designed the home at 53 Janssen Place, and Bert L. Elmer completed construction in 1914. This Mediterranean-style house exhibits both Spanish and Italian influences. The original owner was Granville M. Smith, president of Commonwealth National Bank and member of the cattle-trading firm Smith and Ricker. A subsequent owner installed what is believed to be Kansas City's first elevator in a private residence. (Courtesy of PA.)

The last of the original mansions, 54 Janssen Place was built for the John Wesley Jenkins family. Jenkins owned the J.W. Jenkins Music Company. The home was designed by Shepard, Farrar, and Wiser and was constructed by the Long Construction Company in 1917. The house's Neocolonial Revival architectural features include quoins to define the corners of the house, pediments and decorative railings on the three dormers, a front door bordered with an elliptical fanlight and sidelights, an entrance portico with stone baluster trim, modillions and brackets to define the eaves, and segmented architraves above the windows. (Above, courtesy of PA; right, courtesy of AWSE-KCPL.)

The home at 55 Janssen Place was built in 1911 for William H. Schutz, an ophthalmologist. Distinctive features of this Italianate Revival building include decorative lozenges below the cornice and between the first- and second-floor windows, the arched and columned front door, the stone balustrade, and wide eaves with large brackets. (Courtesy of PA.)

A closer view of the entrance of 55 Janssen Place reveals an intricate iron gate, Doric columns, and decorative antefixes at the top and sides of the arch. (Courtesy of PC.)

After Edna B. Peck's husband died, she moved from a larger Troost Avenue home to 61 Janssen Place. The Joseph Hellman Construction Company built the Neocolonial Revival house in 1909. The architectural firm of Shepard, Farrar, and Wiser designed the structure. (Courtesy of PA.)

The residence at 66 Janssen Place first belonged to the Edward Fouch family. Fouch was vice president of B.R. Electric and Telephone Manufacturing Company. The house was designed by Smith, Rea, and Hovitt and was constructed in 1913 by T.E. Smith. The Jacobean Revival design features an irregular L-shape and asymmetrical facades, dormers, and chimneys. Cut stone frames the windows and caps the brick knee-wall and steps. Brick quoins and timbered gables complete the design. (Courtesy of PA.)

Shepard, Farrar, and Wiser designed 67 Janssen Place. In 1912, John M. Byrne, who lived next-door, reportedly built the home as a wedding gift for his son, Ralph E. Byrne. Did his son and new wife enjoy their proximity to Byrne? The sale of the home in 1915 to Thomas Willock might provide a clue. The Neocolonial Revival style looks modern, with oversized windows, continuous horizontal dormers on the roof, and the sweeping rooflines that characterize a Prairie School–style front porch. (Courtesy of PA.)

John M. Byrne, founder of Byrne Lumber Company, built this 73 Janssen Place home in 1908. The architectural firm Adriance Van Brunt & Brothers designed the house in an Italianate–Neocolonial Revival style with strong Prairie School influences. The lot is one of the largest in Janssen Place. (Courtesy of PA.)

A.H. Glasner, a widow and vice president of Glasner and Barzen Distilling Company, had the 80 Janssen Place house built in 1912. The distinctive design of the Georgian Revival structure was provided by Shepard, Farrar, and Wiser. Glasner spared no expense building her dream home, the cost of which totaled approximately $70,000. (Courtesy of PA.)

The wrought-iron front door and balconies under the windows handsomely set off the buff-colored brick. The distinctive bronze exterior lamps and glass-entrance canopy provide strong architectural focus to the Georgian Revival house's front elevation. (Courtesy of PC.)

The Neocolonial Revival house at 88 Janssen Place features imposing two-story Doric columns across the front veranda. Lynn S. Banks, the general ticket agent for then-new Union Station, contracted with architect Roger Gilman to design the house in 1913. Until 2011, the home served as the residence for the bishop of the Catholic Diocese of Kansas City–St. Joseph. (Courtesy of PA.)

Designed by Shepard, Farrar, and Wiser and constructed by the Carl A. Nilson Company, 96 Janssen Place was built for William C. and Katherine Bowman in 1911. Bowman was founder of the W.C. Bowman Lumber Company. The Neocolonial Revival house features an expansive front porch supported by cast-iron columns. (Courtesy of PA.)

Three

Hyde Park Beautiful

Kansas City's climactic battle in the 1890s was not waged over street railway franchises, gas rates, or even slums. Technically, it centered on the attempt to establish a municipal park and boulevard authority. Actually, its implications were much broader. This struggle involved two basic and opposing concepts of urban life. It was, in short, the old fight between those who think of a city as merely a collection of factories and those who believe that it should be something more.

As early as 1856, Kersey Coates dreamed of a grand boulevard encircling the city. By 1875, with a population over 65,000, there was still no provision for public recreation. In 1881, *Kansas City Star* publisher William Rockhill Nelson started promoting for parks through articles and op-ed pieces six days a week. Powerful supporters joined the campaign, and none was to prove more effective than August R. Meyer, a wealthy nature enthusiast.

In 1893, George E. Kessler and Meyer presented a report to the newly created (1892) Board of Parks and Boulevard Commissioners. The report was based on two basic assumptions: 1) The plan should be not only for present but also for future wants; 2) It is far better to plan comprehensively and broadly and proceed leisurely than to attempt economy in the original plans. By 1895, work on the ambitious plan was underway despite considerable opposition, but by 1900, effective resistance ceased. Without precedent, the 1893 plan grew and expanded with the growth and expansion of the city under the guidance of the creative genius and master direction of one man, Kessler. By 1915, the parks and boulevard system, as it was to stand until after World War II, was virtually complete.

One of the objectives of the system was to connect all the city's different residential districts and establish permanent residential properties, which increased and held their values. Another purpose was to give all residents the opportunity for outdoor recreation as near the homes as it was possible to accomplish. Both purposes were achieved in the Hyde Park neighborhood. Today Gillham Road, Harrison Parkway, Armour Boulevard, and Harrison Boulevard are perfect examples of Kessler's vision and mastery.

George E. Kessler (1862–1923) was a pioneer city planner and landscape architect. His private training in Europe included formal education in forestry, botany, and landscape design. Kessler maintained that touring the major European cities to study civic design was of the most value. Over the course of his 41-year career, he completed over 200 projects in 23 states, 100 cities, and 3 countries. (Courtesy of BPRC.)

Gillham Road, named for Robert Gillham, former park commissioner, is a parkway of varying width, from 75 to 500 feet, and irregular outline extending over hill and through valley. The parkway boundaries have not changed since the land was acquired from private owners from 1901 through 1906. The privately owned park known as Hyde Park was acquired through condemnation in 1902. Gillham Road cost $487,652.92 to acquire, and construction cost $181,911.06. From 1907 to 1910, Kessler prepared general plans for improving Gillham Road. Not all of the plans were implemented. (Courtesy of BPRC.)

Developers of the Kenwood subdivision, fearing shanties in the rugged hollow extending two blocks south of Thirty-sixth Street, turned to George E. Kessler for a solution. In 1887, he designed a private park. With headwaters at Thirtieth Street, Harris Creek drained about one square mile by the time it reached Thirty-ninth Street. During the rainy periods, the creek must have been almost a river, but, otherwise, it was a beautiful little valley, fed mostly by springs. Just south of Thirty-seventh Street, the land leveled out, and the water of Harris Creek spread out into a large shallow bog. Kessler redesigned the park when it was acquired as a part of the Gillham Road condemnation in January 1902. (Both, courtesy of BPRC.)

Hyde Park, as the park was named, revealed Kessler's extraordinary ability to visualize which trees to fell and which to leave, which slopes to smooth, and what naturally dramatic effects of jutting limestone to heighten by carefully cutting, filling, or adroitly placing a curve in an adjacent path or road. By 1910, the tangled undergrowth was replaced with walks, benches, playgrounds, tennis courts, trees, and shrubs. A roadway encircled the park to force the abutting

mansions to face the park. Before it was acquired by the parks department, it was Kansas City's first country club and was surrounded by a high fence and locked gate. When Scotsman Stanley Young introduced golf to area residents, the first golf course was laid down in the park. (Courtesy of Library of Congress.)

In 1904, when these two photographs of Harris Creek were taken, the land was still farmed and undeveloped. At the time, Troost Highlands (1885), Vanderbilt (1886), and Sunny Slope (1902) subdivisions, south of Thirty-ninth Street and west of Troost Avenue, were platted but not yet under construction. The land shown here was acquired by condemnation in 1902 for Gillham Road. The new parkway would run right through the Vanderbilt subdivision. The top photograph faces northwest near Thirty-ninth and Locust Streets, whereas the photograph below faces southeast from about Forty-second and Cherry Streets. (Both, courtesy of BPRC.)

Lots in the Sunny Slope subdivision were just starting to be developed when the top photograph was taken in 1904 from the Harris Creek valley at approximately Forty-fourth and Holmes Streets. The house in the middle on the left is at 4415 Campbell Street. The future subdivision was acquired from the US government in 1834 by Michael Franes and had been included in Westport's annexation to Kansas City in 1897. After numerous transfers, William H. Glaskin bought the property from the James J. Squire's heirs on September 23, 1902, and received development approval seven days later. By 1911, housing along the east side of Gillham Road from Holmes and Forty-fourth Streets south was complete. (Both, courtesy of BPRC.)

Gillham Road between Thirty-ninth and Forty-third Streets contained two sets of roadways. The inner roadway was for fast traffic, while the outer roadways were first bridle paths and later for slower automobile traffic. In this photograph, the northbound automobile is in the west outer roadway. Bridle paths through the parkway were constructed in 1910. A plan by some of the wealthier men to use Gillham Road for buggy races was not received well by other residents. (Courtesy of BPRC.)

The west side of Gillham Road south of Forty-third Street was completed with five sets of stone stairs and pedestrian walking trails. Parts of the hillside were naturalized with extensive tree plantings, and the south end included an open meadow and field area. Part of an original stone wall was woven into the landscape. (Courtesy of BPRC.)

Shown above, the Park Maintenance District No. 2 building was designed by Adriance Van Brunt and Brothers in 1904 and constructed by L. Crosby and Sons a year later. Designed as an "ornamental barn," park employees used it for horse stalls and for storing sprinkling carts and other vehicles. Originally, the barn contained 12 horse stalls, a hospital stall, wagon sheds, harness rooms, an office, and a men's room. It contained the only horse hospital in the parks department. In 1914, additional structures were built (below). The buildings were constructed of native limestone and trimmed with vitrified brick. Originally, the first-floor interior and the courtyard had brick pavement. (Both, courtesy of BPRC.)

George E. Kessler recognized that parks must have buildings for storage, service, and public facilities. He declared that such structures should "never be permitted to become conspicuous either in design or color." Most of his buildings were of native limestone and set back inconspicuously among groves of trees. In 1907, a comfort station (restroom) was built on the west side of Hyde Park near Thirty-seventh Street. The stone, tiled-roof structure cost $2,300. There were also stone steps and a stone wall at the north end of the park. In the 1980s, the restroom was demolished. (Both, courtesy of BPRC.)

This postcard shows road reconstruction, new street trees, and early houses built in the Kenwood subdivision. In the beginning, park roads were oiled macadam pavement. However, the increasing automobile traffic demanded a more cementitiously bonded wearing surface. In 1912, specifications were developed for a bituminous macadam pavement using asphalt as a binder and a very fine spray of oil. (South-West News Company, courtesy of HPNA.)

Land along Gillham Road became highly desirable. In short order, all houses were built, including those on Kenwood Avenue facing the parkway. Craftsman and Bungalow houses provided new owner-occupied housing for middle-class professionals. This postcard shows the intersection of Forty-third Street with Gillham Road and Kenwood Avenue. In 2007, the area was listed in the National Register of Historic Places. (South-West News Company, courtesy of HPNA.)

In the late 1800s, civic leaders were looking for a way to promote Kansas City and encourage visitors. The Flambeau Club started the Priest of Pallas Festival in 1887. This Mardi Gras–style festival included a public nighttime parade and an invitation-only debutante ball organized by a secret society. In the beginning, floats were horse drawn and lighted with kerosene torches. By 1902, the floats were mounted on railway trucks with electric lights. In 1894, the Kansas City Karnival Krewe formed as a humorous event to be held in conjunction with the Priests of Pallas Festival. By 1895, the Karnival Krewe originated the masked ball, daytime street parades, and the flower parade. The first Karnival Krewe festivities also included a band contest, reception, and fire department display. (Both, courtesy of BPRC.)

Ladies chaired the flower parade committee. In 1896, a conservative estimate of the cost of the flower parade, including decoration of carriages, prizes, costuming, and such, was $20,000, the most expensive Karnival week parade. Over 50 professional flower-makers were employed for over a month making flowers. Various church organizations and private circles donated time. In 1903, the Karnival Krewe was discontinued after some activities became too riotous. The Priest of Pallas Festival absorbed its charter and continued some events. Gradually, however, interest in the festival waned, and it ended in 1924. In October 1909, the Fall Festival flower parade was held on Gillham Road. (Above, courtesy of MVSC-KCPL; below, courtesy of BPRC.)

The popular fly-casting pool at Forty-first Street and Gillham Road gave residents a place to practice casting without having to leave town. On certain days, the facility was reserved for children wading. The 1913 casting and wading pool designed by George E. Kessler was rebuilt and enlarged in 1940 and removed in 1976. (Courtesy of MVSC-KCPL.)

Although horse racing was frowned upon, foot races were not uncommon along the Gillham Road "speedway" in 1909. George E. Kessler's plans for improving Gillham Road between Thirty-ninth and Forty-sixth Streets provided for a comprehensive playground, field house, outdoor gymnasium, and ball-field stadium. Unfortunately, there was never sufficient funding to complete the plans. Only the casting pool, tennis courts, paths, and two shelters were completed. (Courtesy of BPRC.)

Harrison Parkway, a branch of Gillham Road, extends two blocks northeast to about Thirty-seventh Street and Harrison Boulevard. This east valley leg was included in Kessler's 1908 and 1910 plans for Gillham Road. This 1907 photograph was taken looking northeast from Thirty-ninth Street. The road on the left originally connected Janssen Place to the parkway but now is a road from the Notre Dame de Sion School. (Courtesy of BPRC.)

Although the date of this photograph is unknown, Gillham Road at Thirty-ninth Street and Harrison Parkway had been graded and oiled, storm drains installed, and the park maintenance building constructed. Left of center is the curve shown in the previous photograph. (Courtesy of BPRC.)

With numerous branches south of Armour Boulevard, Gillham Road is a textbook example of a turn-of-the-century experiment in designing residential areas around parks. The parkway provided not only a central park for neighborhoods but also attractive views for motorists. In 1939, the park provided plenty of area for young boys to ride their bicycles. The man shown below is standing under a tree east of the intersection of Harrison Parkway and Campbell Street. George E. Kessler left many of the sycamores along Harrison Parkway. This tree was estimated to be 100 years old in 1909. (Both, courtesy of BPRC.)

The Harrison Parkway branch of the Gillham Road Parkway demonstrates the innovative parkway design with fluid alignment, bordering roads with houses facing the park land, and intermediate cross streets closed to eliminate intersections. In 1932, the gentlemen shown were standing at the intersection of Campbell Street, Gleed Terrace, and Harrison Parkway. Superintendent of Parks Wilbur Dunn is on the left and Parks Board Commissioner Frank Cromwell is on the right. The center landscape grouping is around the Charlotte Street and Gleed Terrace cave opening, which has since been closed. Charlotte Street does not cross the parkway. Below, Cromwell stands north of Manheim Road and west of Campbell Street. Mayor Bryce Smith's Craftsman-style house is in the background. (Both, courtesy of BPRC.)

The 1893 commissioners report stated, "The object of boulevard construction is two-fold: to provide agreeable driveways, and, by giving certain special advantages and a handsome appearance to such avenues, to make the abutting land, and the land near them, especially sought after for residence purposes, and thereby to enhance the value of such lands." The standard 100-foot-wide boulevard specifications were for a central roadway 40 feet wide and parking 30 feet on each side.

The parking area was to contain 17 feet of turf, then an 8-foot walk, and, between this and the property line, 5 feet of turf. Three lines of trees almost equally spaced were to be planted in this space. Only a few new boulevards met this standard. This panoramic view is Armour Boulevard at Holmes Street. (Courtesy of Library of Congress.)

The plans for South Boulevard were prepared in 1896 and the land acquired in 1899. In 1900, the boulevard was named for Simeon B. Armour, member of the first park board and head of the Armour Brothers Packing House, Kansas City branch. The boulevard was designed according to the standard 100-foot right-of-way. It was widened in 1928, and the curbside row of trees was removed. The 1905 photograph above is facing east along Armour Boulevard from Campbell Street. Below is the view along Armour Boulevard facing west past Harrison Boulevard. (Above, courtesy of MVSC-KCPL; below, courtesy of BPRC.)

Armour Boulevard began as Commonwealth Avenue. After rapid transit systems arrived and land-use restrictions expired in the early 1900s, many of the original mansions were replaced with apartments and hotels designed by some of Kansas City's most prominent architects. Many structures are in the Armour Boulevard Historic District and in the National Register of Historic Places. (Both, courtesy of MVSC-KCPL.)

In 1924, the first Hyde Park Neighborhood Association formed to protest rezoning the east side of Gillham Road from Armour Boulevard south to Thirty-sixth Street. The proposed area would change from single-family status to multifamily or apartment-hotel status. A group of 54 property owners signed a petition protesting the change. Although they were unsuccessful, the new era would bring about the lovely and elegant Hawthorne Apartments shown here at 3515 Gillham Road. (Courtesy of MVSC-KCPL.)

In 1921, Earnest O. Brostrom of Brostrom and Drotts designed the apartment-hotel at 525 East Armour Boulevard. Construction was completed in 1923 by the Armour Building Company. The name was to be *Le Pavonien*, meaning "iridescent or resembling a peacock's train," after the six-foot terra-cotta peacocks surmounting the two entrances. Instead, it became the Peacock Hotel. Then, in 1925, Biene H. Hopkins bought the hotel and renamed it the Newbern. When the two buildings were joined in 1925, Brostrom was again the architect for the one-story barrel-vaulted connecting hall and its terra-cotta ornamentation. The terra-cotta peacocks, which were referred to as "unfortunate 6-foot birds" in a news article of 1925, were said to have offended some hotel guests to the point of turning them away. One of the peacocks, which were removed from the building during the construction, was taken by Brostrom for his garden. The Newbern is architecturally significant as one of the few buildings constructed in Kansas City in the Sullivanesque style. (Courtesy of MVSC-KCPL.)

On August 17, 1927, less than three months after Charles Lindbergh's historic solo flight from New York to Paris, Lindbergh landed his famous *Spirit of St. Louis* aircraft in Kansas City to dedicate the city's new municipal airport. In his speech, Lindbergh praised Kansas City as an important hub for air transportation. The short ceremony was followed by a parade through town. Taken just west of Gillham Road, this photograph shows the parade on Linwood Boulevard. Linwood Boulevard, originally Linwood Avenue, ran almost along the center of the ridge forming the watershed between O.K. Creek (Union Station valley) and Brush Creek. A portion of the avenue was included in the original 1893 parks and boulevards report. The section along Thirty-second Street was designated Linwood Boulevard in 1900. Increased traffic significantly changed the setting of the boulevard. Commercial enterprises replaced older residential buildings, curbside trees were lost, and sidewalks extended to the curb. In 1928, Lindbergh persuaded Trans World Airlines to establish headquarters in Kansas City. (Courtesy of MVSC-KCPL.)

In 1900, Linwood Boulevard was extended along Thirty-second Street between Troost Avenue and Gillham Road. For many years, this section remained residential, with houses, small apartment buildings, and fashionable mid-rise apartment-hotels, such as the LaSalle. Early residents were lawyers, business executives, and physicians. In 1933, a $200,000 ransom was delivered to the LaSalle for a Texas oil tycoon kidnapped by George "Machine Gun Kelly" Barnes. (Courtesy of MVSC-KCPL.)

In 1909, physicians T.W. Thornton and W.E. Minor bought the Lucerne Apartment Hotel at Linwood and Harrison Boulevards for the Thornton and Minor Clinic for treating patients with proctologic disorders. The six-story building was converted into a 300-bed hospital. The hospital merged with another clinic and relocated in 1957, and in 1958, the building became the regional office for the US Department of Veterans Affairs. (Courtesy of MVSC-KCPL.)

Designed by Archer & Gloyd, the Acme Cleaning Company building was constructed at 3200 Gillham Road. The 1925 building featured remarkably ornate architectural details for a commercial/industrial structure, using terra-cotta and other decorative elements. The building was listed in the Kansas City Register of Historic Places in 1983. (Courtesy of MVSC-KCPL.)

Troost Avenue began as an 18th-century Osage Indian trail. The street was named after Benoist Troost, Kansas City's first resident physician. During the 1890s, Troost Avenue evolved from farmland to millionaires row with $135,000 houses, and by the 1910s, it had become completely commercial, the site of Kansas City's first suburban shopping center. (Courtesy of MVSC-KCPL.)

In 1903, the Board of Park Commissioners acquired a portion of the existing Harrison Street. In 1907, surplus trees from nearby Hyde Park were transplanted along the roadway. Harrison Boulevard linked Gillham Road via Armour Boulevard to The Paseo. By 1909, houses had been constructed on approximately half of the lots south of Armour Boulevard. The photograph above shows the coming of the automobile and the going of the horse and buggy. Natural gas lamp standards equipped with Welsbach heads and provided with an extra outside globe of ruby glass were established at a number of boulevard intersections. These lights proved to be excellent regulators and added to the safety of pedestrians as well as vehicle passengers. By 1921, all of the houses had been built. The photograph below was taken from 3516 Harrison Boulevard. (Both, courtesy of BPRC.)

The two central stone walls in this 1911 photograph mark the west and south boundaries of Round Hill, the four-acre estate of Henry C. Flower. In 1925, Flower exchanged the property with the Sisters of Notre Dame de Sion, which began building a new school in 1927. The south stone wall now marks the Gillham Road parkway boundary. The Eagle Scout Memorial was added below the larger pool. (Courtesy of BPRC.)

The Seventh Avenue entrance sculpture to the New York City Pennsylvania Railroad Station contained a clock at the center of a wreath and, depicting day and night, two female figures. In the mid-1960s, the sculpture was donated to Kansas City by the railroad when the station was razed. Architect Maurice McMullen designed the setting and included a fountain to complete the Eagle Scout Memorial. (Courtesy of BPRC.)

Four

Churches, Schools, and Social Clubs

Hyde Park was home to many Kansas City schools, churches, and social clubs. For many settlers, establishing social and cultural institutions was a first priority. In 1906, William Mulkey, an early pioneer, recalled settling in the area when he was four years old in 1828. The Mormons, headed by Joseph Smith, had established a settlement in 1831 with a log cabin school. Mulkey said 12 families attended the small school. He remembered bringing his dinner to school and storing it in Cave Springs (now located along Harrison Parkway), about 100 yards southwest of the school.

The Westport School Board built Hyde Park Grade School to replace the Knickerbocker School. The four-floor brick building cost $24,000 and opened in 1897. Kansas City annexed the school and changed the name to George B. Longan School in 1903. Longan was an early Kansas City school district superintendent. The school building was replaced with a modern structure in 1955.

Westport High School was built when a fire destroyed the old high school. Built by Swenson Construction Co., the brick and stone building cost nearly $500,000. News stories of the day boasted that the school was equipped to teach a boy blacksmithing or a girl cooking and sewing but also offered lessons in Greek and the classics. In a 1910 speech to the student assembly, former president Theodore Roosevelt advised, "Face life as those who play football ought to play football: don't shirk, don't foul, and hit the line hard." Several churches were built at the start of the 20th century. St. James Catholic, St. Mark's Lutheran, Trinity Methodist, and Central Presbyterian Churches were all built at this time and continue providing services and spiritual solace to Kansas City residents.

The largest women's social club in the area was the Kansas City Athenaeum. Formed in 1894, the club built a Greek Revival building at the corner of Linwood Boulevard and Campbell Street in 1914. The club was active in prison reform, public education advocacy, and establishing a juvenile court. Kansas City's first country club was located in the Hyde Park neighborhood. When an early golf course was added, herds of cattle were a natural hazard. Golfers asked the city of Westport to fence roaming cows.

Located near the intersection of Cherry and Thirty-fourth Streets, Hyde Park Elementary School opened in 1897. The first principal was Charles S. Parker, who was also the principal of the earlier frame schoolhouse called the Knickerbocker School. The new four-story brick structure, shown here, cost $24,300 and was designed by F. Middaugh. In 1955, the school was razed to make way for a modern building. (Courtesy of HPNA.)

George B. Longan Elementary, located on the site of the old Hyde Park Elementary School, was built in 1955. Shown here, the building served the neighborhood for over 50 years before it was closed. Most recently, it served as a magnet school in which all classes were taught in French. (Courtesy of MVSC-KCPL.)

Westport High School (located at Thirty-ninth and Locust Streets) opened in the fall of 1908. The architect was Charles A. Smith, and the first principal was S.A. Underwood. The architect designed the school with 60 classrooms, a 1,400-seat auditorium, a gymnasium, showers, a cafeteria, mechanical and domestic science laboratories, and broad stairways. The school cost $440,000. In 1910, former president Theodore Roosevelt spoke to a student assembly. (Courtesy of HPNA.)

In 1927, the Sisters of Notre Dame de Sion moved their girls' school to 3823 Locust Street, shown here. The four-story brick building accommodated grades pre-kindergarten through 12. Many students were daughters of prominent local families. The building contained a swimming pool and gymnasium. History, science, and math were taught in English, but everything else, including fine needlework, penmanship, and playtime, was in French. (Courtesy of Notre Dame de Sion School.)

Shown here is the Junior College of Kansas City, located across the street from Westport High School. Formed in 1919, it was the first two-year college in Missouri to award associate degrees. (Courtesy of MVSC-KCPL.)

Girls from Westport Junior High School are shown playing baseball in the fields north of the school and south of Hyde Park, near Thirty-eighth and Gillham Roads. Neighbors complained to the school about the noise. (Courtesy of MVSC-KCPL.)

In 1894, the Kansas City Athenaeum formed, beginning over a century of service, education, and social benevolence. In 1914, after several years of inventive fundraising, the club completed its clubhouse. The Greek Revival building is located at the corner of Linwood Boulevard and Campbell Street. (Courtesy of Kansas City Athenaeum.)

In 1931, the 30th annual breakfast took place in the Athenaeum ballroom. Over the years, the stained-glass windows and custom-designed matching chandeliers in the ballroom have proved an elegant venue for honored guests, who have included William Allen White, Leo Tolstoy's daughter Iya, William Jennings Bryan, James Whitcomb Riley, and, more recently, Charles Gusewelle and Sheldon Stahl. (Courtesy of Kansas City Athenaeum.)

A Presbyterian church was established in the area by 1857 but did not adopt the name Central Presbyterian Church until later. In 1924, the current building, shown here, was constructed on the corner of Campbell Street and Armour Boulevard. The architectural firm of Shepard, Farrar, and Wiser designed the Classical Revival structure, and Louis Breitag and Son completed construction for $134,390. The Austin Opus 1203 organ was installed in 1924. (Courtesy of Central Presbyterian Church.)

Trinity United Methodist Church, at 620 East Armour Boulevard, is composed of native stone in the English Gothic style. Architects Earnest Brostrom and George Fuller Green designed the church, and the J.R. Van Sant Company built it. (Courtesy of HPNA.)

St. Mark's Lutheran Church is shown here facing east on Troost Avenue. The Lutheran congregation dedicated the $50,000 church, designed by Owen and Payson, on January 16, 1916. The primary facade features crenellated embellishment along the first floor, asymmetrical corner towers with a belfry located in the north tower, and a stepped parapet with a pointed arch and carved limestone cross. Parishioners brought the large stained-glass window from their previous church on Fourteenth and Cherry Streets. The window adorns the primary facade and is the main feature of the sanctuary's balcony. Ten stained-glass windows with limestone tracery and arched heads run along the north and south facades of the church proper. A series of multipaned, double-hung windows make up the north, west, and south facade fenestration of the Tudor-style parsonage. (Both, courtesy of HPNA.)

In 1924, St. Mark's Lutheran Church was expanded by architects Shepard, Farrar, and Wiser. The objective of the design was to preserve the residential nature of the Hyde Park neighborhood to the west. Thus, the restrained character of the west (rear) facade shown here is in sharp contrast to the imposing Gothic Revival style of the east. (Courtesy of HPNA.)

The construction of the new St. James Catholic Church building at 3901 Harrison Street began in 1911. The structure was designed by Sanneman and Van Trump, and construction costs totaled about $40,000. The limestone for the church came from abandoned bridge piers that had stood in the Missouri River. For the cost of dismantling the piers and moving them to the new site, the church obtained enough stone to complete the project. (Courtesy of St. James Catholic Church.)

On July 30, 1929, the parish broke ground for a new rectory, shown here. It was placed directly south of the existing church and was connected by a colonnade. A rose garden was placed between the two structures. (Courtesy of St. James Catholic Church.)

The first Catholic church building was located on the northeast corner of Fortieth Street and Tracy Avenue. The building served as the first school and Sisters of Mercy Convent. After the original school building burned, a new school, shown here, was built in 1924. It was razed in 1977. (Courtesy of St. James Catholic Church.)

St. James was the first tuition-free parochial school west of Chicago. An early photograph is shown above. The Sisters of Mercy from Omaha staffed the new parish school from 1907 until 1972. The school closed a few years later in 1976. (Courtesy of St. James Catholic Church.)

This small chapel at 3801 Gillham Road was built in 1941 as the Pilgrim Lutheran Church for the Deaf. With design roots in historic English country churches, the T-shaped limestone church incorporates Gothic lancet windows, a tile roof, and Gothic ornament. The architect was F.R. Webber of Clifton Ramey, and the builder was Herbert Duncan. (Courtesy of Pilgrim Chapel.)

At the time of dedication, nearly 200 individuals composed the Pilgrim Chapel congregation. The church was designed to be user-friendly. As shown here, the nave included sight lines to maximize the pulpit's visibility. When the sanctuary was full, two sets of doors to the north vestibule could be opened to provide additional worshippers an unencumbered view of the service. (Courtesy of Pilgrim Chapel.)

In the late 1970s, young couples moved back into the neighborhood. The Hyde Park Yacht Club was born as an informal social group with an ironic name. Every month or so, a member would host a party and invite other neighborhood "urban pioneers." At these gatherings, homeowners frequently shared their home-restoration trials and tribulations and the challenges dealing with crime in an unrestored neighborhood. (Courtesy of HPNA.)

Five

Any Housing Style to Suit Your Taste

The first homes in the Hyde Park area were folk-style farmhouses. Several exist today in the Hyde Park neighborhood. When residential development started in the neighborhood, Victorian Queen Anne and shingle styles were arbiters of good taste. Over the years, Colonial Revival, Neoclassical, Craftsman, Prairie, and Tutor styles supplanted the older styles. After World War II, a few ranch homes appeared in the area, but still a walk down any tree-lined street in the Hyde Park neighborhood is a step back in time. It is easy to visualize a slower era when entertainment meant calling on neighbors for a visit on the front porch, arranging a game of croquet, or reading by the parlor fireplace.

In the early days, architects brought the latest East Coast design trends to the Hyde Park neighborhood. Most homes were made of brick or native stone. Many houses incorporated cedar shingles, lap siding, and stucco to very fine effect. Interiors sparkled with leaded, beveled glass doors, windows, and sidelights. In the older Victorian homes, gasoliers and gas sconces were the lighting of choice. A coal-burning fireplace heated nearly every room until the 1900s, when central heating, usually hot-water radiators, became standard, along with indoor water closets and electric lighting. Most homes had hot and cold water in the kitchen and a sink tucked away in a center hall closet where a dusty visitor could freshen up. Bathrooms with toilets were placed on the second and third floors for families and servants, respectively. Larger homes had more bathrooms, often placed between two bedrooms. Closets began appearing in bedrooms, and—in larger homes—in dressing rooms. Many houses featured built-in sideboards, cupboards, and bookcases. Hardwood floors were used throughout the house except in bathrooms and the foyer, where small hexagonal tile was preferred. Hardwood wall paneling and millwork, ornamental plaster features, and crown molding were used extensively for finishing rooms. By the early 1900s, bold colors of paint had replaced elaborate Victorian wallpaper.

The three houses shown here facing south along Thirty-sixth Street (originally Humboldt Avenue) were all built in the early 1890s and had unobstructed views of rolling hills and meadows. The center home belonged to Arthur Stilwell, who planned Janssen Place; the Janssen Place entrance pillars were directly in front of his home. Far removed from the city, the area attracted families of wealth seeking quieter, pastoral settings for their homes. (Courtesy of HKCF-HUD.)

John Barber White and his wife, Emma (Siggins) White, built this shingle-design house on the left in 1892 at 616 East Thirty-sixth Street. The house is pictured on the far right in the photograph above. White's friend Pres. Theodore Roosevelt owned a similarly designed residence at Oyster Bay, Long Island. The style first appeared at seaside resorts in the Northeast and spread to fashionable neighborhoods across the country between 1880 and 1890. (Courtesy of HKCF-HUD.)

The back of 616 East Thirty-sixth Street shows how the shingled upper stories integrated into the lower brick level. The buggy is facing west. The buggy driver is unknown but could be John White's daughter Arabell from a previous marriage. (Courtesy of HKCF-HUD.)

The same horse and buggy appear in front of 616 East Thirty-sixth Street, facing west. Expansive porches were a feature of shingle-style architecture. Other early houses are visible behind the horse to the northeast. (Courtesy of HKCF-HUD.)

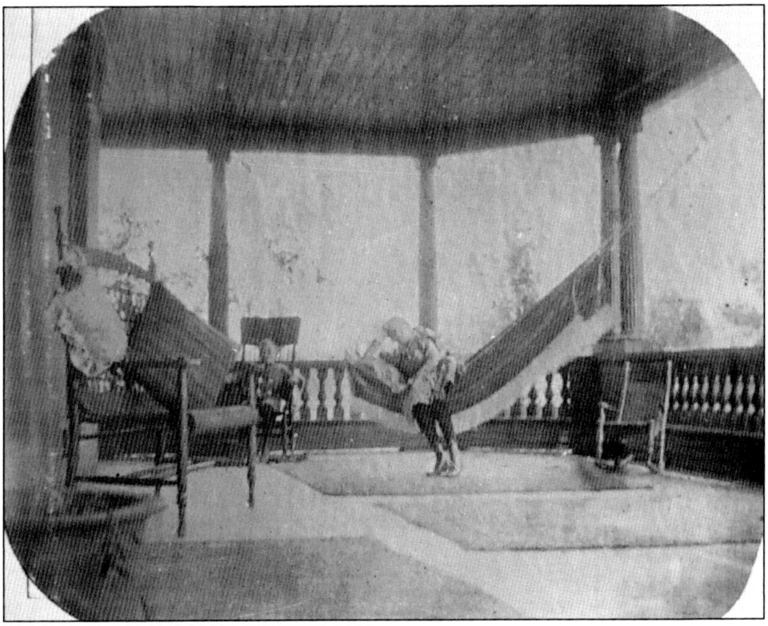

A hammock on the front porch was a welcome refuge during hot Midwestern summers. Emma White's daughter Emma Ruth relaxes on the hammock, and Emma White's son Raymond is in the rocking chair beside his sister. (Courtesy of HKCF-HUD.)

Emma White poses by the front steps with her seven-year-old son Raymond. Classical porch supports were common for the style, but balusters were usually a simple square spindle. (Courtesy of HKCF-HUD.)

The back parlor of the Whites' house is shown above. The piano played an exceptionally important role in the social and cultural life of most middle-class families in the days before recorded music. Small rectangular tile surrounding the fireplace was typical for the period. (Courtesy of HKCF-HUD.)

This is the same room updated a few years later. The piano is now out of sight on the east wall. A new hot water radiator occupies the piano's former position. The drapes and rug are unchanged, but the statuary has changed. (Courtesy of HKCF-HUD.)

The Whites' front parlor was formal, reserved for entertaining guests. The lace curtains are more elaborate than those in the back parlor, and the front window has a floor-length swag included. The ornamental cove ceiling is elegantly finished. (Courtesy of HKCF-HUD.)

Emma Ruth White poses with her doll and buggy in the northwest second-floor bedroom. Born in 1884, Emma was photographed here at about age 13. (Courtesy of HKCF-HUD.)

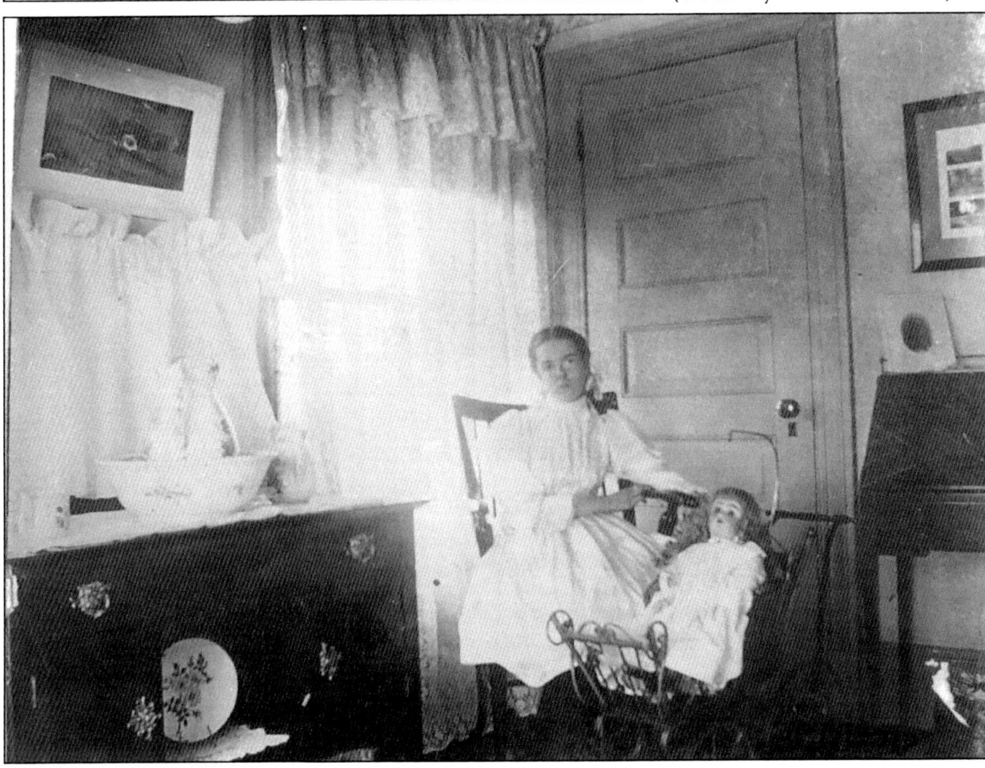

The west facade of 616 West Thirty-sixth Street is photographed here from the second-floor front balcony of the Stilwell house adjacent to the west. In the mid-1950s, the house at 616 was converted into apartments. The porch was enclosed to create more rentable space, and a second-story addition was built over the porch. (Courtesy of HKCF-HUD.)

Emma Ruth White is shown here posing beside a tree. The distinctive porch, which wrapped around the south and west sides, was 616's focal point. (Courtesy of HKCF-HUD.)

Emma Siggins White is photographed with her relative Charles Cardwell McCabe Howe in front of 616 West Thirty-sixth Street. This picture provides nice details of the front porch and the sunburst over the front steps. An imposing globular light fixture is suspended behind the pair. (Courtesy of HKCF-HUD.)

In this gathering on the front steps, Emma Siggins White sits between two ladies. Raymond White is on the far left, and next to him may be his older half-brother John Franklin White, born in 1875. The latter studied to become a physician but died tragically by accidental gunshot in 1900. The flowering clematis and emerging cannas are still popular landscape plants in Hyde Park. (Courtesy of HKCF-HUD.)

Bicycles became popular among the middle and upper classes in the 1890s. The new "safety bicycle" was the first design suited for children and women. This period was considered the golden age of bicycles. They became an important means of transportation and a popular form of recreation. Bicycling clubs for men and women spread across the United States, including Kansas City. (Courtesy of HKCF-HUD.)

A billy goat is harnessed to a cart of neighborhood kids. Many early residents of Hyde Park kept domestic animals for eggs, milk, meat, and fun. (Courtesy of HKCF-HUD.)

By the late 1970s, the house at 616 East Thirty-sixth Street had been divided into multiple apartments. The expansive front porch was enclosed to provide more rental space, and additional rooms were built over it. The interior was also divided. (Courtesy of HKCF-HUD.)

This street view shows the 616 East Thirty-sixth Street house after it was restored in 1986 to its original design. The Historic Kansas City Foundation bought and restored the structure with the support of Hyde Park residents. (Courtesy of PA.)

Pictured above is 3659 Charlotte Street, a frame-and-stone house with half-timber decorations and stucco infilling between the timbers. Gustave Bachman and his wife, Madge Bryant Bachman, built the house in 1907. The Bachman family moved to Kansas City after the Civil War. Gustave was vice-president of his brother-in-law George Peck's dry goods store. Madge Bryant Bachman's family were early settlers, owning a 40-acre farm in what is now downtown Kansas City. This eclectic Tudor-style home features a prominent stone chimney and elaborate flue cap on the home's south side. Below, the white pergola at the southwest corner lends a Craftsman motif, as do porch supports on the east entry and decorative braces under the gables. (Both, courtesy of Doug and Susan Borge.)

The back of 3659 Charlotte Street is shown before the house was renovated in the 1980s. The atypical attached garage is on the left. The fire escape was a code requirement dating from the house's conversion to a multifamily dwelling. Most large homes in Hyde Park bore a similar fate during and after World War II, when Kansas City experienced a housing shortage. (Courtesy of Doug and Susan Borge.)

The house at 720 East Thirty-sixth Street was built in 1906 in the Arts and Crafts style. The unusual entrance and design is the work of architect John McKecknie. Joseph Layton and Eleanor Harmon Mauze lived here in 1930. He was a clergyman at Central Presbyterian Church in Hyde Park and author of numerous divinity papers. (Courtesy of HPC-KCMO.)

The architectural firm Owen and Payson designed this 1914 Neoclassical-style house at 711 Manheim Road. Thomas T. Crittenden Jr. and his wife, Mason, were the first occupants. This symmetrical facade entrance, typical of the style, is dominated by a full-height porch roof supported by columns in the classic style. The estimated cost was $10,000. Crittenden was mayor of Kansas City from 1907 until 1910. He died in 1938, but the house remained in the Crittenden family until the late 1940s. By the late 1950s, the house was a multifamily dwelling. Details of the threshold are shown at right. (Both, courtesy of Catherine Thompson and Paul Hansen.)

Shown here is the unique brickwork of 711 Manheim Road. The unusual double chimneys and parapet gable roof also characterize the west facade. The first-floor windows are set in blind brick arches with diamond designs. All the windows and doors have stone lintels. (Courtesy of PA.)

The stone, wood, and shingle home at 3520 Holmes Street was built in 1906 for John and Marguerite Sullivan. This eclectic Colonial Revival (also known as Dutch Colonial) home includes Victorian and shingle features, such as an eyebrow window between gambreled gables, third-floor Palladian windows, and bay windows on the first two floors. (Courtesy of Kate McNeive.)

The French-Eclectic-Norman house at 3727 Holmes was built in 1909 for about $20,000. Striking features include a green tile roof, arched and hipped dormers, steeply pitched and flared roofs and eaves, and an asymmetrical facade. The Colonial Revival veranda, with its broad sweep and classic supports, lends appealing counterpoint. An arched roofline and prominent circular porch on the right suggest a main entrance, but the threshold is actually on the left of the porch aligned with the steps in the top view. Below is a view from the side. (Both, courtesy of Paul and Debbie Stevermer.)

Architect Shelby H. Kurfiss originally designed 3727 Holmes Street for J. Sidney Smith. Kurfiss also designed the homes at 3719 and 3733 Gillham Road and 3707 Holmes. Smith never lived in the house and sold it to Louis Oppenstein in 1910. Oppenstein (1875–1938) moved to Kansas City in 1902 and opened a jewelry store, Oppenstein Brothers. Shown below from the veranda facing east, the park provides a pastoral view. The porch shown was demolished during the 1960s but was restored to its original splendor in 2011. (Both, courtesy of Paul and Debbie Stevermer.)

The back of this asymmetrical home features a prominent round tower with a high conical roof. The exterior walls are stucco. A three-car garage with chauffeur quarters on the far right was part of the original design. The transition from carriage house to garage came quickly in the early 1900s. (Courtesy of Paul and Debbie Stevermer.)

The focal point of the spacious center hall at 3727 Holmes Street is the stairway. The living room, which opens up to the restored veranda, is shown to the right. On the left (unseen) is a doorway to the dining room and kitchen. Most of the woodwork is mahogany. (Courtesy of Paul and Debbie Stevermer.)

The Colonial Revival house at 3538 Harrison Boulevard was designed by John W. McKecknie (1862–1934) in 1907 for James H. White, owner of the Baltimore Shirt Company. McKecknie came to Kansas City in 1898 and began his own architectural firm in 1901. The heavy cut-stone front porch and the asymmetrical veranda were unique features, shown above. In the days before central air conditioning, sleeping porches were necessary during steamy Kansas City summers. The home was equipped with a modern icebox. Each day the iceman delivered a large block of ice. Shown below, the access door to the icebox is clearly visible to the right of the back porch door. (Both, courtesy of Patrick and Jane Alley.)

Many of the homes in Hyde Park have ornate plaster ceilings. This living room ceiling at 3538 Harrison Boulevard is a lovely example. John McKecknie designed a number of homes in Hyde Park, including 419 and 720 East Thirty-sixth Street, 3511 Locust Street, 3652 Charlotte Street, 3326 Campbell Street, 3900 Holmes Street, and 7 Janssen Place. Shown at right is a detailed close-up of the quarter-sawn white oak paneling and the two-foot ornate crown molding in the dining room. Most of the molding is plaster, although the small dental blocks are wood, as is the lowest ogee. (Both, courtesy of Patrick and Jane Alley.)

The dominant feature of the French Eclectic house at 3521 Holmes Street is the imposing slate hipped roof and symmetrical facade. Double-hung windows with stone lintels and sills regulate the space. A Palladian window is centrally placed but almost obscured by the classical entrance. Elaborate cornices and quoins nicely frame this yellow-brick structure. Two circular copper dormers with oeil-de-boeuf (bullseye) windows complete the front facade. The house was built in 1906 for Louis and Anna Knoche Tippe. The architect was Selby Kurfiss. Below, the south side porch has classical columns and, above, a detailed entablature. Interior woodwork is mostly quarter-sawn white oak. (Both, courtesy of PC.)

Frederick C. Gunn designed this 3530 Harrison Boulevard house in 1911 for Gardner Mercantile Company owner David Gardner and his wife, Lyda. The estimated cost of this stone residence was $10,000. Here, vernacular construction drew heavily on the Prairie style, shown by the one-story porch, massive porch supports, natural materials, low-pitched roof, and wide eaves. (Courtesy of David and Kathy Disney.)

Frederick C. Gunn, born in 1865, practiced architecture with Louis Curtiss in 1890. The partnership lasted until 1898. The firm was successful from the beginning, designing the Missouri State Building for the 1893 World's Columbian Exposition in Chicago and the Progress Club and Virginia Hotel, both on Washington Street in the Quality Hill neighborhood. Gunn designed General Hospital, City Market, and the National Fidelity building. He died in 1959. (Courtesy AWSE-HKCF.)

A.A. Mosher, a local railroad executive, had this Victorian house built in 1892. The house, at 600 East Thirty-sixth Street, was constructed of red brick and Colorado sandstone and had a red slate roof. Queen Anne features included patterned masonry, wall texture differences, stone and terra-cotta decorative wall panels, and patterned masonry chimneys. In the late 1970s, the house underwent extensive restoration to reemphasize its elaborate cherry and oak woodwork, six fireplaces, cut-glass windows, two pantries (one for the butler and one for the cook), and turreted "tutoring room" off the second-floor landing. Of particular note is the high carriage step on the west side of the house and the elaborate first-floor carved stone fireplace. (Above, courtesy of HPC-KCMO; below, courtesy of PA.)

Sam Swerengen and his mother Lizzie Swerengen built this Craftsman-style home at 4411 Gillham Road in 1907 for about $4,000. Hipped-roof Craftsman homes are rare and are similar to the American Foursquare Craftsman style but differ with respect to the exposed rafters, the protruding window treatments on the left side, and the window box under the eaves. (Courtesy of PC.)

This home at 3440 Campbell Street was built in 1899 for Frank Askew and his wife. Farrow Architects designed the home. Distinctive exterior features are the asymmetrical porch leading to the entrance at the side of the house and the bold treatment of stone and brick on the street-facing chimney. (Courtesy of HPNA.)

American homebuilding changed dramatically from 1865 through 1900. Home pattern books featuring floor plans and stock-milled house parts became widely available. They were developed to provide rural working families affordable houses. Simple Homestead-style or temple-form homes, such as 4021 Holmes Street shown above, were popular architectural choices. Plat maps published in 1891 confirm that this house was already in place by 1890. As seen at left, original features included bullseye trim framing the doors and windows and matching stained-glass windows in the front door and window. Two-story construction provided maximum floor space under a single roof. The straight walls and gables were easy for part-time carpenters to build. Minimal ornamentation reduced construction time and cost and kept maintenance to a minimum. (Both, courtesy of HPNA.)

Architect George Bastman and his wife, Elizabeth, lived at 4021 Holmes Street from 1912 until 1950. This house was not connected with city water until 1950, and then it was done only to make the property salable after Elizabeth died. (Courtesy of HPNA.)

The home at 816 Armour Boulevard was built for Samuel E. Sexton, president of Hucke and Sexton Contracting and Building Company. The 1905 French Beaux Arts house was constructed of stone and brick. An atypical brick size (1.5 by 14 inches) distinguishes this house from other Hyde Park brick. The unique proportions accentuate the horizontal lines of the home. (Courtesy of HPNA.)

This Kansas City shirtwaist dwelling at 3331 Harrison Street is a regional adaptation of the gabled Prairie house subtype. The wood-frame house is clad with different exteriors. The first floor is stone, while the second level is shingled. The term "shirtwaist" was coined for the unique central flare where the upper floor meets the lower, much like women's dress style of the day. The Cowherd Brothers Construction Company built the home in 1900. (Courtesy of Doug and Susan Borge.)

The home shown here, built by Cowherd Brothers in 1900, is located at 3335 Harrison Street. The shirtwaist home sold to Anton Weber in 1901 for $7,700. Relatively affordable, the house nevertheless contained rich architectural materials and details. (Courtesy of Patrick and Marsha Depping.)

The stone structure at 416 East Thirty-sixth Street was built for attorney Delbert J. Haff, an early proponent of the Kansas City parks and boulevards system. It was designed by architect Walter C. Root and built in 1901. The property was landscaped by George E. Kessler, the master designer of Kansas City's renowned parks and boulevard system. The Colonial Revival house features a symmetrical facade, multiple-paned windows, and half-timber detailing in the gables, shown above. Classical columns are at the entrance to the music room, the main stairway (shown below), and surrounding windows in the library. Six varieties of wood were incorporated in the interior. Leaded and pieced glass is found on windows, French doors, and pocket doors. The house is believed to be the first in Kansas City built with an air-conditioning system. The early method forced air over blocks of ice in the basement through interior ductwork. (Above, courtesy of HPNA; below, courtesy of PC.)

The west side block of 4300 Campbell Street was developed in 1905 and photographed here shortly thereafter. The houses shown below and on the next page are all visible in this photograph. A close look reveals a few residents enjoying the day from their front porch. (Courtesy of Brad and Marilyn Rine.)

Constructed in 1905, the residence at 4330 Campbell Street is a two-and-a-half-story brick and clapboard American Foursquare. Characteristics that mark the style include the box shape, flat exterior, natural materials, bell-cast hipped roof and dormers, and full-length front porch. (Courtesy of HPNA.)

Jessie Runcie and his wife, Anna, purchased 4300 Campbell Street and lived here until 1940. Runcie was president of Western Paper Box Company. The house is a two-story shirtwaist style with Craftsman detail, like all the other houses on the 4300 block of Campbell Street. (Courtesy of HPNA.)

This shirtwaist-style home at 4304 Campbell Street and the identical home in the photograph above were both built in 1905. (Courtesy of HPNA.)

The cut-stone vernacular house at 743 Manheim Road shown above was built for Mack Barnabas and May Nelson about 1907. Nelson was an executive with the Long-Bell Lumber Company. The Nelsons sold the home to George Muehlebach in 1915. Muehlebach owned the Kansas City Blues baseball team and built Muehlebach Field (Kansas City Municipal Stadium). Muehlebach also built the Hotel Muehlebach. The first floor has beautiful woodwork, bay windows, and leaded, beveled glass. At left is the home's original bathroom pipework and showerhead. The basement still contains an original fireplace. (Above, courtesy of DRB; left, courtesy of HPNA.)

In 1908, the home at 3521 Harrison Boulevard was built for $8,000. This stone-foundation Craftsman-influenced house was built with steel I-beam supports and exterior walls three bricks thick. Special features included an eight-foot-wide built-in lighted hutch and window seats. George and Caroline Fuller were the second owners; Fuller was on the board of parks and boulevards, and Caroline was the first woman elected to the Kansas City School Board. (Courtesy of Bill and Dona Boley.)

John Hayes, the first owner of 3521 Harrison Boulevard, was born on July 4, 1855. He moved to Kansas City in 1872 and joined the police force in 1880, becoming chief of police in 1897. In 1900, when the Democratic National Convention was held in Kansas City, Hayes presided over security. After he left the police department, he operated a very successful detective agency with his son. (Courtesy of AWSE-HKCF.)

In 1911, this Colonial Revival house at 3601 Charlotte Street was built for Benjamin Berkshire, an executive with Berkshire Lumber Company. The brick house was designed by Shepard, Farrar, and Wiser and incorporates multiple architectural styles. The main entrance and colonnaded front porch face south, away from the street. (Courtesy of DRB.)

This residence at 3525 Harrison Boulevard was designed in the Colonial Revival style by Shepard, Farrar, and Wiser and built by Joe Hellman in 1908. The first owner was Mortimer R. Platt, who was in the banking and livestock trades. At the time of construction, the Colonial Revival style referenced early English- and Dutch-built residences along the Eastern Seaboard. (Courtesy of HPNA.)

After the early 1900s, fireplaces were no longer the primary heat source. Hot-water radiators, such as that shown under the window at 3525 Harrison Boulevard, provided the homes with heat. Most houses of the period retained one or more wood-burning fireplace for ambiance, a century-old trend that continues today. By the 1950s, many Hyde Park homes were divided into apartments, usually seven units. Most of the first-floor woodwork was painted. In this home, restoration began in 1979 with the arduous removal of paint from the extensive woodwork on the first floor. As shown below, Colonial Revival homes in Hyde Park usually included fanlights and sidelights around the front door. (Both, courtesy of HPNA.)

The dining room of 3525 Harrison Boulevard, the finishing of which is clearly Craftsman, is graced by pocket doors and beveled-glass windows with stained-glass panes. In the late 19th century, the term Colonial Revival actually described a hybrid design of many styles. Purely Colonial-style houses were rare. The term is applied based on the exterior facade. If it has accented crowns and pilasters or if the entrance extends forward and has columns and a porch, it is called Colonial regardless of the interior treatments. (Courtesy of HPNA.)

This Colonial Revival residence at 737 Manheim Road was constructed in 1907 and purchased by John and Lola (Sweet) Tennant in 1913. Tennant was vice president of the Long-Bell Lumber Co. The house's symmetrical lines seen are emphasized by the position of two chimneys, one over each side gable, and the three front dormers. (Courtesy of HPNA.)

Shown above is a later photograph of the 737 Manheim Road front entrance, now painted. The large windows on each side of the doorway are decorative leaded, beveled glass. (Courtesy of PA.)

This 1909 Colonial Revival house at 500 East Thirty-sixth Street was built for attorney Frank Brumback and his wife, painter Louise (Upton) Brumback. It was designed by Lewis S. Curtis, a prominent Kansas City architect. Curtis designed several hundred buildings locally, but few are in Hyde Park. He was known for progressive designs in the tradition of Frank Lloyd Wright. (Courtesy of HPC-KCMO.)

The 1910 shirtwaist home shown at left was designed and built by G. E. Shelton at 904 East Forty-second Street for about $2,000. Shelton also lived in the house. The two-story stone and shingle residence sits high above street grade, making it appear taller. The terrace garage was added in 1916 and then lengthened beneath grade in 1963 to accommodate longer cars. The oak front door with beveled-glass and stained-glass sidelights is original to the house. (Courtesy of HPNA.)

This distinctive keyhole-design stone fireplace highlights the foyer and living areas inside 904 East Forty-second Street. Decorative milled oak trim surrounds the doors and windows throughout. A 21-pane window in the living room is repeated in the dining room, which also features a bay window and box-beam ceiling. (Courtesy of HPNA.)

This 1905 stone, stucco, and shingle shirtwaist home, located at 3665 Harrison Boulevard, was built for Frank Barhydt and his wife, Susie (VanDyck) Barhydt. Frank was manager of Kansas City's American Type Founders Co. The garage behind the house is a much simpler, utilitarian structure than were earlier carriage houses. Gone also are the chauffeur's quarters above. Below, Susie Barhydt poses behind the wheel of the new family car in 1924. By then, horses were gone from Hyde Park, and the preferred mode for going downtown was to ride on the Troost Avenue Street Car. (Both, courtesy of Gary and Jane Foltz.)

In the days before air-conditioning, the front porch of 3665 Harrison Boulevard was the place to read and socialize in the summer.The late-August-afternoon photograph above shows Frank Barhydt reading a book on the front porch. Times were simpler in 1924, but that did not mean that people were not careful about appearances. Barhydt, shown below, is busily at work in his front yard watering some shrubs. His preferred gardening attire appears to be a coat, tie, and vest. (Both, courtesy of Gary and Jane Foltz.)

From left to right, neighborhood boys Ernest Pringils, Bobby Pringils, Billie Wallace (with the dog), and Frank G. Barhydt (grandson of Frank Barhydt) pose with Ernest and Bobby's dog. Two wear knickerbockers, which are baggy, knee-length trousers common in the early 20th century. Three boys wear flat newsy caps, which have largely been replaced by today's ubiquitous baseball cap. (Courtesy of Gary and Jane Foltz.)

Local architects Wilder and Wright designed this classic Prairie School cut-stone-and-stucco house at 3800 Campbell Street in 1907. Prairie is one of the few indigenous American styles. It is part of the first phase of the Modern tradition of architecture, the Arts and Crafts movement. This style began in Chicago under the leadership of Frank Lloyd Wright. The entrance is off-center and inconspicuous. The fireplace in the living room contains Rookwood tiles in shades of red and brown, no two of which are the same. (Courtesy of HPC-KCMO.)

Architect C.M. Jesperson designed the residence at 3728 Holmes Street. The home was built in 1924 for Victor Speas. This brick Prairie School features a symmetric, tiered elevation. The prominent entrance faces Harrison Parkway. A hipped roof with a dominant one-story side porch characterizes the style. Speas prospered in the juice and vinegar industry. His lifestyle might have been unconventional for the time and place. He was devoted to his mother, who lived with him until her death. Speas dated the same woman for 30 years. Shortly before his mother died, Spears married at age 64. (Above, courtesy of PA; below, courtesy of HPNA.)

In 1905, the home at 3600 Harrison Boulevard was built for attorney James Henry Harkless and Carrie M. (Kiser) Harkless. He was born in Ohio in 1856 and became a member of the Kansas City bar in 1886. This striking American Foursquare home was constructed of natural stone. The red-tile hipped roof and imposing stone wall add to its immense appeal. (Courtesy of HPC-KCMO.)

Root and Siemens designed this cut-stone Tudor residence at 642 East Thirty-sixth Street in 1905 for W.W. Sylvester, vice president of Kansas City, Mexico, and Orient Railroad. He lived in the house only a year. Tudor elements are apparent in the arch drip molds over the third-floor windows and the lancet windows in the upper sashes of the dormers and third-floor windows. (Courtesy of DRB.)

This 1889 residence at 3608 Campbell Street is one of the oldest in the area. It was built for Frederick O. Rugg, a lumberman. His business partner, John Harmon, owned an adjacent house. The Queen Anne structure, which is missing much of the ornate trim and towers associated with the design, may have been a Sears kit house. The front porch on the right side is distinctive. The house also features stained-glass windows. (Left, courtesy of Pam and Jeff Gard; below, courtesy of PC.)

Six

Fighting Back

In many American cities, 19th-century upper-class neighborhoods deteriorated as the affluent residents moved away. The Hyde Park neighborhood experience was similar, as the younger well-to-do populace gravitated to upscale housing in new parts of town. During and after World War II, a housing shortage developed. As older affluent homeowners died, their houses were converted to multifamily apartments. The character of the neighborhood changed; gentility gave way to rental landlords interested in full occupancy, not in maintaining buildings or historical context.

During the civil rights movement in the 1960s, racial tensions escalated, especially after race riots broke out in Kansas City following Martin Luther King's assassination. Many white residents fled urban cores to suburban areas beyond the fray. Although Hyde Park experienced no physical damage, white flight decreased home values to unprecedented low levels. In the early 1970s, the low prices and the large and lovely old homes began attracting a new generation of young couples, married, single, or gay.

They encountered roadblocks in the form of redlining by lenders, which meant buyers could not get loan approval for properties in the neighborhood. To surmount this barrier, the neighbors organized and brought political pressure on city hall. The first meetings were in late 1973, and within two years, the Hyde Park Neighborhood Association was fully formed and operational. A misguided perception of Hyde Park schools also created barriers. While the public grade schools and Notre Dame de Sion provided quality education, a lingering reputation deterred potential buyers. Real estate agents showed no interest in suggesting the area to potential home buyers.

To combat these misconceptions, the Hyde Park Neighborhood Association began organizing annual homes tours starting in 1977. Attendance increased yearly, and by the early 1980s, more than 10,000 people attended the two-day festival. The tours were enormously successful in redeeming perceptions of Hyde Park. Between 1975 and 1980, housing prices doubled, and by 1985, they doubled again.

The home tour and festival continues today. The 2012 tour will be the 30th anniversary. Once again, Hyde Park is the lovely and comfortable community it was intended to be. Glory restored, it has reestablished itself as a Kansas City jewel.

Water and fire damage and decay are just a few of the misfortunes that occur when old homes are neglected. Deterioration usually starts with the roofs, which eventually causes damage throughout the house. (Courtesy of Catherine Thompson.)

Another old-house peril is the remodeling urge of previous owners. They modernized windows and siding, split up rooms, lowered ceilings, and enclosed porches. Below is a house whose Foursquare character is compromised with inappropriate vinyl siding; small, misplaced windows on the second floor; and no windows on the first-floor front; but it does have two front doors! Most restorations start by undoing what others have done. (Courtesy of PA.)

When homes in Hyde Park were converted into multifamily dwellings, exteriors were altered by attaching outdoor fire escapes and staircases, like this house at 3717 Harrison Boulevard. Porches were often removed and chimneys were neglected. (Courtesy of HPNA.)

Homes were abandoned as they deteriorated. Their interior fixtures were sold, and the houses were left open to the elements and the indigent. They became eyesores to the neighborhood and destroyed property values. (Courtesy of HPNA.)

All houses in Hyde Park suffered the consequences of neglect. Vinyl siding was installed, and ornate eaves and window trim were removed or replaced with modern materials. (Courtesy of Pam and Jeff Gard.)

In the 1970s, the tide began to turn for Hyde Park. The new residents organized and reclaimed their streets from the criminal elements. Street fairs and homes tours were organized, as shown here. (Courtesy of PC.)

New young owners had more energy than money. The renovation work was largely do-it-yourself projects. It was not hard to find owners working on their house. Architectural salvage stores and thrift shops were haunts for homeowners looking for hardware and fixture to replace. (Above, courtesy of PC; below, courtesy of PA.)

The second year of the home-tour festival saw large increases in the numbers of people appreciating older homes. Neighbors solicited the support of local and national politicians. Tom Eagleton, a US senator, attended the festival (center of the group on the driveway). (Courtesy of PC.)

Some of the tour attendees were older Kansas City residents who had lived in Hyde Park as children. Other visitors were younger families from the suburbs considering a move to Hyde Park. (Courtesy of PC.)

The early festivals replicated the turn-of-the-century lifestyle. Neighbors dressed in period clothes and provided horse-and-buggy rides. (Courtesy of PC.)

The festivals were also a party for the neighborhood. (Courtesy of PC.)

Hundreds of people were recruited as volunteers to act as tour guides, sell tickets, and serve food and drinks. Brochures provided information and detailed histories of each home on the tour. (Courtesy of PC.)

Festivals lasted two days, and most residents contributed time and encouraged their friends to attend. (Courtesy of PC.)

Picnics took place across the majestic lawns of the mansions on Janssen Place. People from all around joined in festivities. (Courtesy of PC.)

Early urban pioneers, like Tom Becker, provided the festival transportation from house to house. Drivers offered historical information and enumerated the benefits of living in Hyde Park. (Courtesy of PC.)

BIBLIOGRAPHY

As We See 'Em, a Volume of Cartoons and Caricatures of Kansas Cityans. Pen-and-ink sketches by D.P Thomson. Kansas City, MO: H.B. Thomson, Lechtman Printing Co.

Diamond Jubilee 1892–1967, A Story of the Development of the Parks and Recreation Department. Kansas City, MO: Kansas City Parks and Recreation Department.

Haskell, Henry C. Jr. and Richard B. Fowler. *City of the Future, A Narrative History of Kansas City, 1850–1950.* Kansas City, MO: Frank Glenn, 1950.

Lee, Janice, David Boutros, Charlotte R. White, and Deon Wolfenbarger. *A Legacy of Design: An Historical Survey of the Kansas City, Missouri, Parks and Boulevards System, 1893–1940.* Kansas City Center for Design Education and Research. Columbia, MO: University of Missouri–Columbia, 1995.

McAlester, Virginia and Lee McAlester. *A Field Guide to American Houses.* New York: Alfred A. Knopf, 1984.

Miller, Patricia Cleary. *Westport Missouri's Port of Many Returns.* Kansas City, MO: Lowell Press.

Report of the Board of Park & Boulevard Commissioners of Kansas City, MO. Kansas City, MO: Hudson-Kimberly, 1893.

Whitney, Carrie Westlake. *Kansas City, Missouri: Its History and Its People 1808–1908.* vol. 3. Chicago: S.J. Clarke, 1908.

Wilson, William H. *The City Beautiful Movement in Kansas City.* Kansas City, MO: The Lowell Press, Inc., 1964.

The Hyde Park Neighborhood Association was formed in 1969 and incorporated as a not-for-profit corporation in 1974. There is a 13-member board headed by a president. Except for a brief period, the organization has been completely supported by volunteers. The association has hosted homes tours since 1977 and published a neighborhood newsletter since 1975.

When first organized, one of the immediate concerns was to bring the neighborhood into compliance with current city zoning ordinances. In recent years, because of the association's efforts, much of the neighborhood has been rezoned to single-family. It also reached out to real estate agents and banks to increase the availability of home loans for the area.

The association, working with city council members, has been able to obtain over $2 million in public improvements. Improvements have included reconstructing part of Gillham Road, curbs, and sidewalks; adding over 200 parkland trees; historic stone step repairs; and new playground facilities. In addition, hundreds of volunteer hours have been donated to remove invasive plants on park land. Since 1976, the association has led the effort to plant over 800 trees. In 1987, it won the Governor's Town Treescape Award for the planting of over 385 street trees.

The Historic Kansas City Foundation awarded the Hyde Park Neighborhood Association Historic Homes Tour the Proactive Preservationist 2001 Preservation Award. The award notes: "The Hyde Park Neighborhood Association has conducted historic homes tours for 23 years. Over 150 homes and churches have been showcased, all with volunteers. This effort by HPNA has promoted a resurgence of investment not only in Hyde Park but also in other historic neighborhoods in Kansas City. The success of these tours is an ongoing testimony to the value of grassroots preservation."

The association has worked hard to be recognized for its historic structures. The following items are listed in the National Register of Historic Places: six districts, five buildings, and three individual houses. (Logo courtesy of HPNA.)